CONTENTS

 @lfc  @liverpoolfc   liverpoolfc TikTok @liverpoolfc

Editor David Cottrell **Assistant Editor** William Hughes **Writer** Chris McLoughlin **Production** Michael McGuinness, Roy Gilfoyle, Adam Oldfield **Design**, Lee Ashun, Colin Sumpter, Glen Hind **Photography** Alamy, Mirrorpix, Liverpool Echo, John Powell, Andrew Powell, Nicholas Taylor © Liverpool Football Club & Athletic Grounds Ltd **Published by** Reach Sport
Managing Director Steve Hanrahan **Commercial Director** Will Beedles **Executive Art Editor** Rick Cooke **Executive Editor** Paul Dove
Marketing & Communications Manager Claire Brown **Website** www.reachsportshop.com **Printed by** Buxton Press

standard chartered
standard chartered
standard chartered
L.F.C.

WEMBLEY WINNERS

The League Cup is much maligned in some quarters but you try telling that to success-crazy players, staff and fans who have just seen the club make history AGAIN

#CARABAOCUPFINAL
TSIMIKAS
21
HENDERSON
14
058
BROADCAST
Carabao Cup

LIVERPOOL
FOOTBALL CLUB
WE ARE LIVERPOOL
WINNERS
2022
Carabao
ENERGY DRINK

WINNERS 2022
Carabao ENERGY DRINK
RED ZONE

THANK YOU
FOR YOUR SUPPORT
Carabao ENERGY DRINK
standard chartered

Carabao ENERGY DRINK

LIVERPOOL FOOTBALL CLUB
EST. 1892
Carabao ENERGY DRINK
Standard Chartered
L.F.C.
WINNERS 2022

LIVERPOOL FOOTBALL CLUB
Carabao

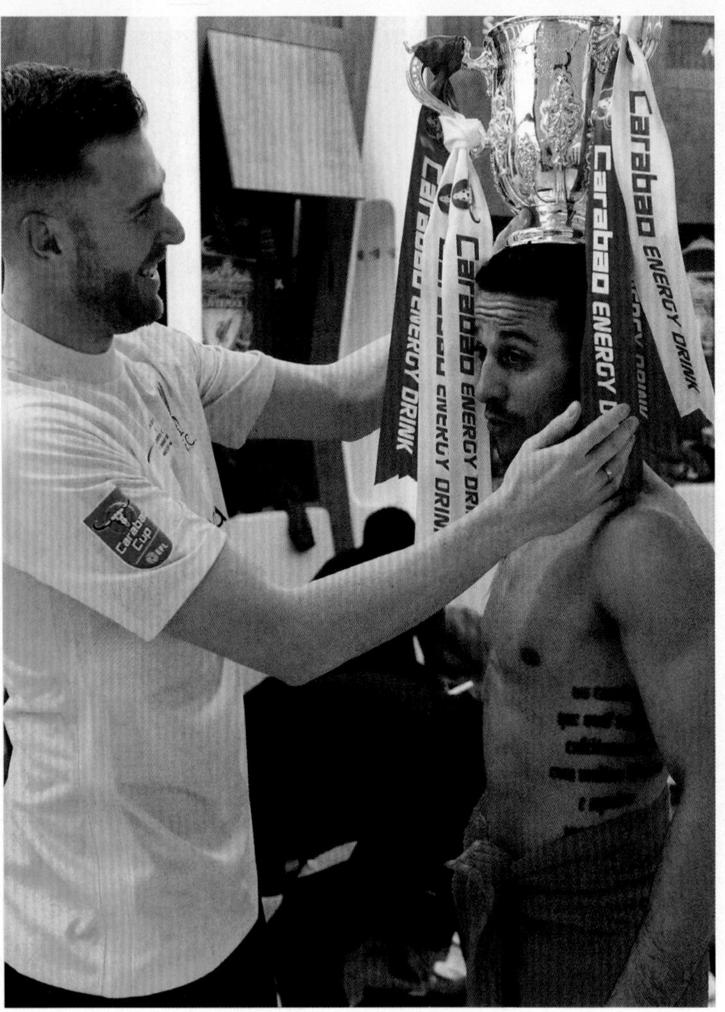
Carabao ENERGY DRINK

L.F.C.
WINNERS
Carabao ENERGY DRINK

Adrian
Henderson
Oxlade-Chamberlain
Minamino
Diogo J.
Tsimikas
Luis Diaz
Robertson
Origi
LIVERPOOL
FOOTBALL CLUB

Carabao ENERGY DRINK

ALEXANDER-ARNOLD
66

'After the game it was nice to celebrate with the people after a long time without having any reason to celebrate'

WORDS OF WEMBLEY WINNERS

JÜRGEN KLOPP

"We were here and lost a final in a penalty shootout like six, seven years ago. Afterwards nobody talks about it, it's like, 'You were twice at Wembley and you lost both finals'. It was a tight game, we were clearly better in the second half against Man City that time. We should have won it in the second half, didn't, and then in the shoot-out we lose. As a professional sportsperson, that's life. So now, in 10 years' time, nobody will ask, 'How did you win exactly against Chelsea?' You just have to win it. Were we better tonight than that time against City? I'm not 100 per cent sure, to be honest, but we are more experienced, that's a massive difference. We don't get nervous when things don't go well. We really keep our nerve.

"The start of the game was clearly better from Chelsea but all of a sudden, we were really in the game and then we let them run and we were the clear dominant team. I'm not sure 100 per cent but the first half was like 63 or something [per cent] possession – against Chelsea that's not that easy, so there was a lot of good football stuff obviously. But over 120 minutes you cannot hold them back and away from your goal, so they had their chances and obviously they scored 'goals' more than us, but they all were offside. That's pretty harsh to take for them I can imagine but I'm really happy about the effort and all these kind of things and yes, it's a big one for us because it's the first time for this group but the ninth time for the club, which is very important as well.

"Our fans were obviously quite happy about the whole thing tonight, the atmosphere was outstanding, I really loved it. And after the game it was nice to celebrate with the people after a long time without having any reason to celebrate something, or not the opportunity to celebrate something. So, I'm really happy about the whole thing.

"Facing Chelsea, there was like two lions going for each other – it was absolutely crazy. Then the penalty shoot-out, one of the most spectacular I ever saw. Absolutely great to win it like this. We called it the people's cup but the whole journey was a squad journey and that's what I love most about it."

WORDS OF WEMBLEY WINNERS

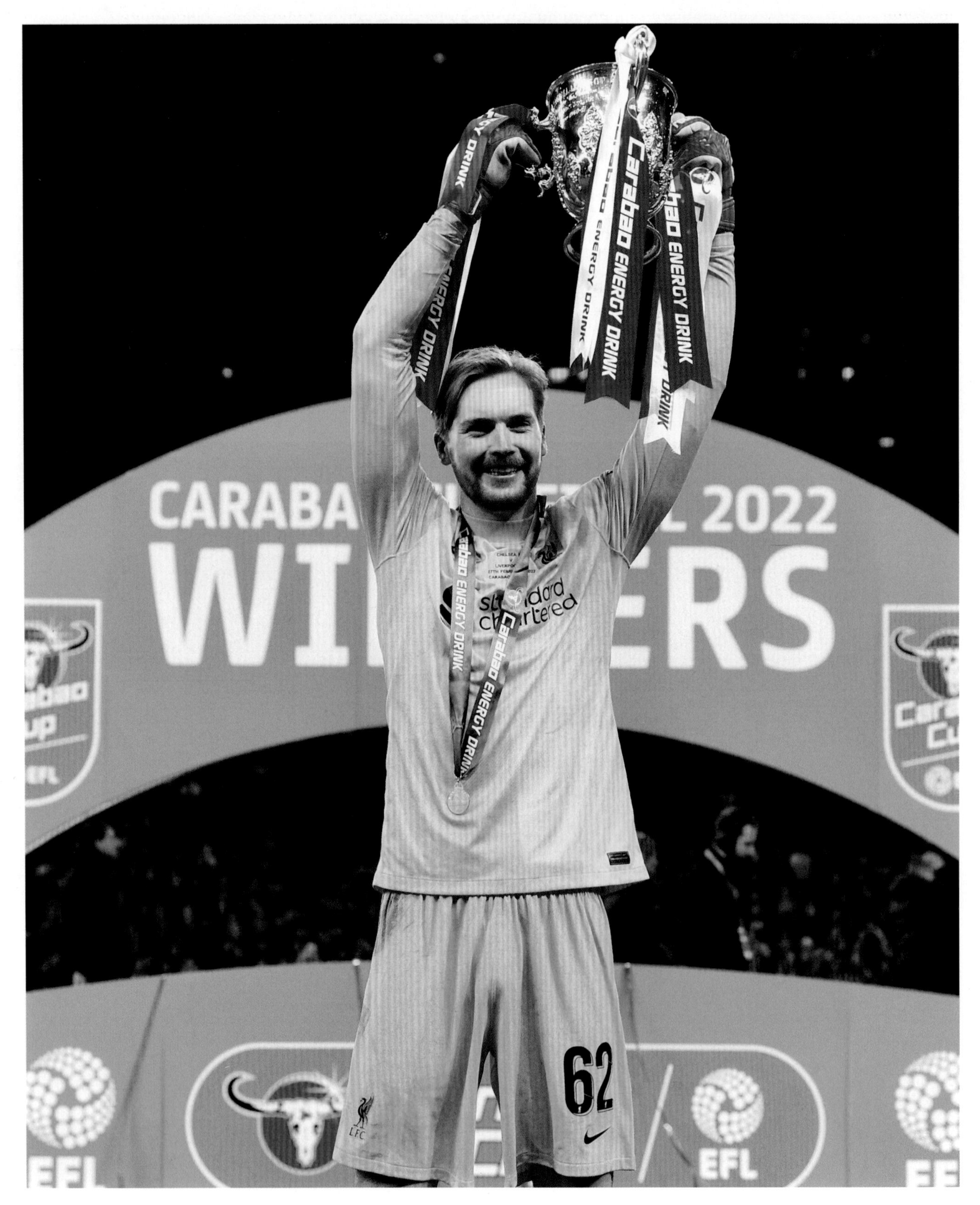

CAOIMHIN KELLEHER

"Someone said to me afterwards, 'You scored the winning penalty' but I wasn't really bothered about that and I was more bothered that I wanted to make a save! But, thank God, anyway I scored and we got the win.

"I was dreaming good things last night, that we would win, but never in my wildest dreams would I have thought I'd score a penalty at the Liverpool end, the winning penalty. That's just next level.

"He [Alisson] is brilliant. You saw Chelsea change their goalkeeper at the end as well, so for me to get the faith from the manager was special and Ali has just been great with me. There was no sulking or anything like that, he's totally focused and he has been really helpful for me."

JORDAN HENDERSON

"It's very special to win trophies for this football club, no matter what the competition. It was a great opportunity for us and thankfully we were on the right side of it. It's always difficult when it goes to penalties; it's never nice. But I thought the lads deserved to win overall.

"It's really pleasing that we've used all of the squad from the start of the competition – players from the first team and academy have all chipped in, which makes it even more special.

"I never take for granted playing for this football club and how special that is – and to be winning trophies is extra special. The fans deserve it, the players deserve it. It was a fantastic day and hopefully this can give us a little kick-start for the last few months of the season because there's a lot of football to be played."

ANDY ROBERTSON

"I was desperate for him [Kelleher] to save one, especially when I knew mine was coming up. I was so desperate for him to save one! His pen was ridiculous. That's where I think penalty shoot-outs are horrible – when it gets to the end it's lads that are the least confident and don't really want to take one and they sometimes decide the finals. But Caoimh's penalty was different class. The most important thing was we won it, whatever way we were willing to do it, whatever way possible. It had to go to penalties and luckily we all scored ours.

"It has been really tight between us and Chelsea all season. The two games in the Premier League have both been draws. Today, we both had chances; I think they probably had the better chances, to be honest with you. Quite an open game, but I think by the end everyone was just knackered and I think you could just see both sets of teams were kind of looking at each other thinking, 'When will this end?' It's really tough on the body, a lot of work has been put into this. The longer it goes, somebody has to miss a penalty and it's horrible really. But, fortunately, it wasn't one of our lads."

EST·1892
Carabao ENERGY DRINK
Carabao ENERGY DRINK
Carabao ENERGY DRINK

VIRGIL VAN DIJK

"The games we've played against Chelsea have always been very intense so it was expected but we're just very happy that we got the trophy. It gives us something to build on for the rest of the season.

"There were outstanding penalties from all of us. Under full pressure everyone did well. We practised them quite a bit.

"At Liverpool we are all a family and we do things together. The atmosphere today was outstanding and we're all very happy. Credit to all the players who have been involved, from the youngsters who started the competition to the players who haven't played as much of the league campaign – so everyone has been a part of this.

"I'm very happy for Caoimhin. It will give him a boost of confidence and it will make him more mature to play the way he played at this level."

CHELSEA 0
LIVERPOOL 0 (after extra-time)

LFC won 11-10 on penalties

27.02.22 • Wembley • Attendance: 85,512

Referee: Stuart Attwell

CHELSEA (3-4-3): Mendy (Arrizabalaga 120); Chalobah, Silva, Rudiger; Azpilicueta (James 57), Kante, Kovacic (Jorginho 106), Alonso; Mount (Lukaku 74), Pulisic (Werner (74), Havertz. **Subs not used**: Sarr, Niguez, Loftus-Cheek, Hudson-Odoi.
Booked: Kovacic, Kante, Havertz.
Penalties scored: Alonso, Lukaku, Havertz, James, Jorginho, Rudiger, Kante, Werner, Silva, Chalobah.
Penalties missed: Arrizabalaga.

LIVERPOOL (4-3-3): Kelleher; Alexander-Arnold, Matip (Konate 91), van Dijk, Robertson; Fabinho, Henderson (Elliott 79), Keita (Milner 80); Salah, Diaz (Origi 97), Mane (Jota 80). **Subs not used:** Alisson, Tsimikas, Oxlade-Chamberlain, Minamino.
Booked: Alexander-Arnold.
Penalties scored: Milner, Fabinho, van Dijk, Alexander-Arnold, Salah, Jota, Origi, Robertson, Elliott, Konate, Kelleher.

REPORT BY WILLIAM HUGHES

HOW IT HAPPENED...
EVERY BIT OF ACTION FROM THE REDS' LEAGUE CUP FINAL TRIUMPH

Before kick-off Liverpool captain Jordan Henderson and his Chelsea counterpart Cesar Azpilicueta show solidarity with the people of Ukraine by carrying yellow and blue wreaths as part of the Football Stands Together statement.

The Reds are dealt a late blow when midfielder Thiago Alcantara has to withdraw after sustaining an injury in the warm-up. The Spaniard is replaced in the starting 11 by Naby Keita with Harvey Elliott coming into the squad on the bench. A tearful Thiago is seen in the moments before kick-off being consoled on the sidelines by Alisson Becker.

4.30pm - The final gets underway with the Reds attacking the end opposite their own supporters.

3 - Chelsea mount the first attack and try to release full-back Marcos Alonso down the left but good covering from Trent Alexander-Arnold sees the ball go out for a goal-kick.

6 - A big chance for Chelsea. Front man Kai Havertz glides across the pitch and releases Azpilicueta, whose low cross is met by an effort from unmarked winger Christian Pulisic in a central position. Liverpool keeper Caoimhin Kelleher produces a fine save to paw away his effort with a strong left hand.

8 - Free-kick to Chelsea after a foul by Fabinho on Azpliicueta. Midfielder Mason Mount delivers the set piece and defender Antonio Rudiger stabs an effort wide at the far post but is then flagged offside.

12 - Luis Diaz does well down the left and finds Sadio Mane. He tries to pick out someone out on the right but the ball is hacked clear by Rudiger. Mane then weaves his way past defender Trevoh Chalobah but his effort is blocked by centre-back Thiago Silva.

16 - A fine double block by Reds centre-back Joel Matip denies efforts from Mount and fellow midfielder Mateo Kovacic.

17 - Andy Robertson finds Mane down the left. He is half-stopped by Chalobah but is back on his feet quickly to try and pick out a team-mate but Thiago Silva clears Chelsea's lines.

18 - Alexander-Arnold's cross from the right picks out the lively Mane, who ghosts between defenders Chalobah and Azpilicueta, but the Senegalese attacker, playing as the Reds' central striker, misdirects his header across the area rather than at goal.

20 - Virgil van Dijk's long ball picks out Luis Diaz who produces fine control before finding Mohamed Salah, whose shot is blocked.

21 - Mount's foul on Mane gives the Reds a free-kick on the edge of the box.

22 - Alexander-Arnold flicks the free-kick into the path of Salah but he cuts across his shot which swerves well wide of Edouard Mendy's goal.

23 - Chelsea midfield anchor N'Golo Kante attempts to find Havertz but the pass evades the German and drifts wide of goal.

24 - Robertson again links up well with Diaz down the Liverpool left and he wins a corner off Chalobah.

26 - Alexander-Arnold tries to find Mane but the ball runs through to Mendy.

27 - Robertson's cross from the left is deflected behind for a corner by Azpilicueta. From the dead ball, Van Dijk flicks the ball on at the near post and the Reds appeal for a penalty after it strikes Azpilicueta on the arm but the defender knew little about it and referee Stuart Attwell waves play on.

28 - Mane wins a corner on the right but nothing comes from the flag kick.

30 - Mane slips the ball to Keita on the edge of the area. His low drive is saved by Mendy. Mane is quickest to react but he is denied by a stunning stop from point-blank range by his international team-mate who completes a fine double save.

34 - Fabinho's shot from distance is blocked by Kante and the ball rolls harmlessly through to Mendy.

35 - A chance for Chelsea as Pulisic's throughball releases Havertz and as Kelleher comes out to narrow the angle, he dinks a shot wide of the target. The German is then flagged offside anyway.

37 - Robertson's deep cross from the left is headed wide by Salah at the back post under pressure from Alonso.

39 - Pulisic's shot is parried by Kelleher and as the ball is crossed back into the area, it is headed well clear by Van Dijk.

40 - Van Dijk's quick free-kick releases Diaz down the left and he forces a corner.

42 - Azpilicueta plays a one-two with Havertz on the edge of the area but the defender's left-footed shot flies high over the bar from 25 yards.

45 - A big chance for Chelsea on the stroke of half-time as Pulisic finds Havertz on the right edge of the box. His cross finds Mount in space and he somehow drags his shot wide of the target when in on goal. The assistant referee raises his flag but replays suggest Mount was onside.

45 - One minute of additional time is played before referee Attwell brings a close to the opening period.

Half-time: Chelsea 0 Liverpool 0.

5.32pm - The second half gets underway with both sides now attacking the ends housing their own supporters.

48 - Havertz finds space down the left to put a cross in but Pulisic can't reach it at full stretch.

49 - Chelsea hit the post. Havertz beats Joel Matip in a wide area and finds Mount in space and the midfielder is one-on-one with Kelleher. After a good first touch, the ball seems to get stuck under his feet and his stabbed effort strikes the upright before rolling across the face of goal and the Reds are able to clear to safety.

52 - Diaz tries to chip a pass through to Mane. Mendy is out quickly to punch the ball to safety.

54 - Diaz stretches the Chelsea defence and after twice twisting his way past Chalobah, the Colombian wins a corner on the left.

57 - Injury forces Azpilicueta off the field and he is replaced by Reece James.

58 - Alonso and Havertz combine to release Mount, whose shot is saved by Kelleher, who grabs the ball at the second attempt as Pulisic closes in.

60 - Chalobah and Keita clash as they contest a challenge and both men require treatment after nasty knocks.

63 - Alonso wins Chelsea's first corner of the game after a raid down the left.

65 - A big chance for the Reds. Mane slides the ball into the run of Salah who advances in on goal, but his dinked effort over Mendy doesn't quite have the required pace on it and Thiago Silva runs back to clear by the goalline. It all emanated from a poor clearance by the Chelsea keeper.

66 - Liverpool win a free-kick on the right after Salah is fouled by Alonso.

67 - The Reds think they have taken the lead as Alexander-Arnold's free-kick is headed back across goal by Mane and Joel Matip heads home at the back post. The goal is given and Liverpool celebrate but the decision is referred to VAR and referee Attwell is sent to the TV monitor by VAR official Darren England. He then disallows it after adjudging Van Dijk to have blocked off James in an offside position.

70 - Diaz does well down the left from Mane's pass but Thiago Silva clears his cross as Keita closes in.

73 - A double change for Chelsea. Striker Romelu Lukaku replaces Mount and fellow attacker Timo Werrner comes on for Pulisic.

75 - Alexander-Arnold tries to pick out Salah but his pass is overhit.

76 - Diaz is set away down the left and runs in on goal. He outpaces Chalobah but his shot from a tight angle towards the near post is saved by the legs of Mendy.

78 - Chelsea think they have broken the deadlock but their celebrations are cut short. Diaz is caught in possession and Werner's cross is headed in at the back post by Havertz but he is flagged offside. Replays show both Werner and his Germany team-mate Havertz are offside when Kovacic plays the initial pass forward.

79 - A triple change for the Reds as Harvey Elliott replaces skipper Jordan Henderson, while James Milner also comes on for Keita in midfield and takes the captain's armband. Diogo Jota takes over from Mane in attack. The Diogo Jota song rings out from the Liverpool fans.

82 - Milner plays a one-two on the edge of the box with Salah but his shot on the stretch goes high over the bar.

84 - Kelleher does well to keep Matip's back-header in play and prevent the Reds from conceding a corner.

85 - A deep cross by Salah is headed out for a corner by Chalobah.

85 - Robertson's cross from a short corner almost sees Diaz and then Matip turn the ball in but Chelsea scramble the ball clear.

88 - Chelsea break forward and Kante's cross towards Werner is defended superbly by Alexander-Arnold who heads clear.

89 - Salah breaks clear and is pulled back on the halfway line by Kovacic who receives the first booking of the game.

90 - Jota wins a corner from Thiago Silva on the right.

90 - Fourth official Andrew Madley's board shows that six minutes of added time will be played.

90 - Van Dijk's header from a powerful Alexander-Arnold corner is well saved by Mendy.

91 - Werner's effort is blocked by Alexander-Arnold.

92 - Jota wins another corner as his shot is blocked at the near post after a sliced clearance by Thiago Silva.

94 - A superb save from Kelleher denies Chelsea a late winner! Alonso's cross from the byline is directed goalwards by Lukaku but the Irishman flicks out his left foot to produce a vital instinctive save.

96 - Kelleher's goal-kick marks the end of normal time.

Full-time: Chelsea 0 Liverpool 0

90 - Ahead of extra-time Liverpool make a change with Ibrahima Konate replacing Matip.

6.28pm - Extra-time kicks off with both slides attacking the same ends as in the first half of normal time.

93 - Robertson overhits a pass down the left and Diaz can't keep it in play.

94 - Werner attempts to curl a shot in as he cuts in from the left of the area but his effort goes too high.

96 - Werner dribbles across the box from left to right and finds Kante but the Frenchman drives high over the bar.

97 - The Reds pep up their attacking options with Divock Origi replacing Diaz.

98 - Chelsea have another effort disallowed. A pass finds Lukaku in the inside right position and he cuts inside Konate before firing past Kelleher at the near post, but replays show the Belgian is in an offside position. VAR upholds the original decision to chalk off the 'goal'.

99 - N'Golo Kante goes into the book for tugging back Jota.

102 - Van Dijk does well to get a good clearing header on a dangerous cross delivered in from the left by Alonso.

105 - One minute of added time is played.

105 - Both Alexander-Arnold and Havertz go into the book after an altercation which sees the players square-up after a tangle of legs in getting up following a sliding challenge by the Reds' right-back.

Half-time: Chelsea 0 Liverpool 0.

106 - A change in the holding midfield role for Chelsea as Jorginho replaces Kovacic.

106 - Kelleher is out quickly to the edge of his box to gather as James attempts to find Lukaku with a throughball.

107 - Alonso finds space down the left and his attempted cross is blocked for a corner by Konate.

107 - The resulting flag kick is punched clear by Kelleher under pressure from Rudiger.

108 - Jorginho tries to find Lukaku but his pass is just too strong as Konate holds off the Chelsea attacker and Kelleher is quickly out to gather.

109 - Chelsea have a third goal disallowed as Havertz fires a smart angled drive into the far corner from Lukaku's cross after racing in behind Alexander-Arnold. He is again rightly ruled to have strayed into an offside position.

112 - Milner attempts to find Jota but the Portuguese attacker can't take the ball cleanly in his stride as he advances on the Chelsea penalty area.

113 - Elliott's low cross into the box lacks power and is comfortably gathered by Mendy.

115 - Salah forces a mistake out of Rudiger in the box but is unable to get a shot away as the centre-back makes a fine recovery challenge.

115 - Lukaku runs away from Fabinho down the left and crosses towards Werner in the box, but Van Dijk gets himself in a good position to clear.

116 - Werner tries to get clear of Konate in the box but the Frenchman recovers well to concede a corner.

118 - Robertson's low cross from the left picks out Jota who peels away to make space but is unable to make proper contact with his shot.

119 - Alexander-Arnold's chip towards Origi looks dangerous but the Belgian is unable to bring it under his spell and the ball runs out for a goal-kick.

120 - Chelsea boss Thomas Tuchel makes a big call with the game heading towards penalties, replacing Mendy with sub keeper Kepa Arrizabalaga.

120 - One minute of additional time is applied at the end of extra-time.

120 - Kelleher clears well after Konate plays a back pass to him to see off pressure from Lukaku.

121 - Stuart Attwell blows the final whistle and the destination of the trophy will be decided via a penalty shoot-out.

James Milner wins the toss for ends and a big cheer goes up as the shoot-out takes place in front of the Liverpool supporters.

The Reds' players stand near the centre circle ready for the drama from 12 yards while Chelsea boss Tuchel crouches in the middle of a huddle to address his players.

7.10pm - Milner steps up to take the first penalty as a rendition of 'You'll Never Walk Alone' rings out among the Liverpool fans. Milner hits his shot to his left and sends Arrizabalaga the wrong way. 1-0.

Marcos Alonso walks up to the spot to huge boos from the Reds fans. He hits his effort to his right and scores despite Kelleher going the right way. 1-1.

Fabinho steps up and referee Attwell warns Arrizabalaga for his antics in coming off his line to try and distract the Liverpool player. The calm Brazilian dinks a 'Panenka' penalty over the keeper. 2-1.

Romelu Lukaku sends Kelleher the wrong way as he goes to his right. 2-2.

Virgil van Dijk steps up. He goes to his left and although Arrizabalaga goes the right way, the Dutchman's shot is too high and powerful. 3-2.

Kai Havertz stops in his run-up before going to his right to send Kelleher the wrong way. 3-3.

Trent Alexander-Arnold is next up and scores with a good penalty to his left despite Arrizabalaga guessing the correct way. 4-3.

Reece James has to score to keep Chelsea in it and does so, going to his left to find the net. 4-4.

Mohamed Salah. The Egyptian makes it 5-4 as he slots home to his right.

Jorginho makes it 5-5 after 10 penalties with his trademark jump and side-footed effort which sends Kelleher the wrong way.

Diogo Jota begins the sudden death element of the shoot-out as he goes down the middle to score. 6-5.

Antonio Rudiger scores as he hits his effort just to the right of the middle. 6-6.

Divock Origi goes down the middle to find the net. 7-6.

N'Golo Kante sends Kelleher the wrong way as he shoots to his left. 7-7.

Andy Robertson sends Arrizabalaga the wrong way to make it 8-7.

Timo Werner levels it up again at 8-8 as he fires home to his left.

Harvey Elliott shoots to his left and sends the Chelsea keeper the wrong way. 9-8.

Thiago Silva nets an assured penalty as he goes to his left to make it 9-9.

Ibrahima Konate's effort goes to his right and although Arrizabalaga gets a hand on it, the shot has enough power to find the net. 10-9.

Trevoh Chalobah makes it 10-10 meaning the two keepers will be up next!

Caoimhin Kelleher shows why he played as a striker in his younger days as he slots home confidently, sending Arrizabalaga the wrong way. 11-10.

Arrizabalaga steps up and spots the ball. He then skies his shot high over the bar to give the Reds an astonishing 11-10 shoot-out success and confirm the Redmen's 49th major trophy.

Dua Lipa's hit 'One Kiss' rings out over the public address system as the Liverpool players celebrate jubilantly in front of their fans.

Just before 7.30pm, Jordan Henderson and his team-mates climb the Wembley steps before being presented with the cup. Henderson performs his fifth trophy lift as LFC captain and the celebrations begin!

STATS

CHELSEA		LIVERPOOL
11	SHOTS	20
4	ON TARGET	6
45%	POSSESSION	55%
544	PASSES	638
76%	PASS ACCURACY	79%
14	FOULS	10
3	BOOKINGS	1
7	OFFSIDES	1
2	CORNERS	11

WE LIVE FOR DAYS OUT

BY CHRIS McLOUGHLIN

One miss is all it takes, falling in love with Quive...

As the travelling Kop celebrated Liverpool's Carabao Cup final penalty shoot-out success with Dua Lipa's 'One Kiss' ringing out over the Wembley PA system, Caoimhin Kelleher was engulfed by his team-mates close to the corner flag.

Kelleher had scored Liverpool's 11th penalty, sending Kepa Arrizabalaga the wrong way. The Chelsea keeper, brought on specifically for the shoot-out, then sent his spot-kick into orbit. With such simplicity the Carabao Cup was won.

The 23-year-old Irishman had made history as the first Liverpool goalie to win three penalty shoot-outs. Unusually, he didn't make a save, yet scored the winning kick.

Maybe playing as an outfield player as a teenager was crucial. Perhaps his unflappable, calm demeanour put him in good stead. Or maybe, as Jürgen Klopp said afterwards, Kelleher is simply the best number two goalie in the world and his decisive contribution was just what he does.

A clean sheet plus a winning penalty in a League Cup final is legendary stuff and skipper Jordan Henderson recognised it when he told Kelleher to take the cup and show it off to the photographers congregated on the Wembley sideline. His family album will need some extra pages now.

Whether 'Quive' should have started ahead of Alisson was the subject of much discussion as Kopites descended on Wembley.

LIKE THIS

Scarves hanging from car windows fluttered in the wind on the M6 and M1. Motorway service stations were Red. So too were the trains down to London Euston.

Liverpool supporters live for days out like this. With all due respect, the Carabao Cup will never go ahead of the Premier League, Champions League and FA Cup in terms of priorities, but no club has won it more than the Reds and winning it was celebrated like it meant the world.

Truth be told, the travelling Kop were in good voice all over the capital all day. The beer garden in the Green Man – one of the pubs allocated to Reds supporters – had so many LFC banners draped outside they could have done with a washing line.

'MY LIVERPOOL THE KOP WILL ALWAYS RULE' read one. 'MENTALITY MONSTERS' and 'JURGEN'S REDS MATE' read others. 'UKRAINE YNWA' was the most poignant.

It is only four years since Kopites were in Kyiv for the Champions League final and there was a huge show of solidarity for Ukrainians and what they are going through. Banners, placards and flags – displayed by supporters of both clubs – got the message across, as did some chants and a period of supportive applause before kick-off.

Liverpool supporters chanted 'You'll Never Walk Alone' towards the end of that period and they meant it. Memories of the fan park in Shevchenko Park – and Dua Lipa playing 'One Kiss' – before kick-off in the 2018 Champions League final remain fresh in the mind. Some things are more important than football.

Over on Kilburn High Road, the North London Tavern echoed to the sound of the Diogo Jota and Virgil van Dijk songs, while across the way the Brondes Age pub had more of those distinctive red and white lettered banners draped outside it. Scousers here, Scousers there...

Wembley Way was chocka. Seas of Red and Blue made the pilgrimage towards the arch, their precious tickets tucked away. The concourses were busy and loud; the queues for drinks and the loos lengthy.

Ahead of kick-off, two giant banners featuring both teams in comic book style were unfurled on the pitch and after a show of solidarity for Ukraine the action got underway.

Wembley atmospheres are always different. Supporters are so spread around the stands that you never get a nucleus of singers a la

The Kop, more sporadic chants emerging in multiple areas. Chelsea fans waved their plastic flags, Liverpool supporters covered their end in homemade banners. After all those months when football was played behind closed doors it felt like everyone was owed a day out and a cup final. Not that you'd watch the 120 minutes again if goals are your thing.

It was scrappy, but both sides had their chances – Edouard Mendy denied Naby Keita and Sadio Mane, while Kelleher saved from Romelu Lukaku. The shrewd judges had anticipated extra-time and penalties and they were right, but not before some dramatic moments.

Joel Matip had a goal disallowed for a foul by Van Dijk, Romelu Lukaku had one chalked off for offside. Mason Mount struck a post, Mo Salah's chipped finish was cleared off the line. So it went to spot-kicks and, after travelling Kopites sang YNWA again and joined in with some of the tunes played by the Wembley DJ (ex-Red Gini

Wijnaldum's chant rang out while Tiesto's 'The Business' was aptly timed) before arguably the finest cup final penalty shoot-out of all followed as all 20 outfield players converted.

Kelleher almost saved a couple. Fabinho's dinked finish was bullish, and even Harvey Elliott – Liverpool's youngest cup finalist who wasn't in the squad when it was named, but got his chance after a tearful Thiago was injured in the warm-up – slotted his peno home like a pro.

So it came down to the keepers. Kelleher stepped up and sent Arrizabalaga the wrong way. Arrizabalaga stepped up and sent the ball flying over the bar, just like Charlie Adam in 2012.

Liverpool were Carabao Cup winners for a record ninth time and the celebrations were wild. Henderson led his men up the Wembley steps before doing a 'Hendo shuffle' as he lifted the cup, which was passed along the line to every man to raise aloft. The celebrations continued on the pitch – Klopp swapping his fist-pumps for cup lifts – and into the dressing room where footage of the post-match party went viral.

Mo Salah was photographed holding his medal. Man-of-the-match Van Dijk chilled with the League Cup on one knee and the Alan Hardaker Trophy on the other. Yes lads, Naby Keita posted a video on Instagram stories live. Carabao Cup debutant Luis Diaz sat pointing at the cup as he celebrated being the most successful Colombian footballer in Merseyside football history. Most of the squad bounced around the dressing room.

It was a joyous night, but it felt like the start of trophy-gathering, not the end.

The aim now is to turn one trophy into two, three or even four. For Jürgen Klopp's class of 2021/22 this might just be the beginning – and the catalyst – for a truly special season.

While it took 120 minutes and 22 penalties to secure another piece of silverware, sometimes one miss is all it takes...

A BIG DAY OUT AT ANFIELD SOUTH

It had been a long time since Liverpool fans had been able to enjoy being part of a huge Wembley occasion in a major domestic cup final – so you just knew the best supporters in the world would be ready to make the most of it!

CONGRATULATIONS LIVERPOOL
L.F.C.

CUP FINAL
CUP FINAL

KICK-OFF
16:30

L.F.C.
Standard Chartered

LIVERPOOL
FOOTBALL CLUB
EST. 1892

CHELSEA
FOOTBALL CLUB
V
CHELSEA v LIVERPOOL

standard chartered
Expedia
62

standard
chartered
EFL
Carabao
Cup

standard chartered
standard chartered
standard chartered
EFL
EFL

LIVERPOOL FC
CARABAO CUP
WINNERS 2021/22

LFC
standard chartered
standard chartered
LFC

YOU'LL NEVER WALK ALONE
LIVERPOOL
FOOTBALL CLUB
EST·1892
LIVERPOOL FC
CARABAO CUP
WINNERS 2021/22
NAL 2022
ERS
Carabao
Cup

CARABAO CUP
Carabao Cup

JURGEN KLOPP
LIVERP

KONATÉ
5
HENDERSON
14
standard chartered
LFC

WHEN SEPTEMBER COMES

NORWICH CITY 0
LIVERPOOL 3

Goals: Minamino (4, 80), Origi (50)
21.09.21 • Carrow Road • Attendance: 26,353
Referee: Darren England

NORWICH (3-1-4-2): Gunn, Omobamidele, Hanley (C), Gibson, Rupp, Mumba (Rashica 69), Gilmour, Lees-Melou (Dowell 77), Giannoulis, Tzolis (Pukki 69), Idah.
Subs not used: Krul, Kabak, Sorensen, Williams.
Booked: Lees-Melou, Rupp.

LIVERPOOL (4-3-3): Kelleher, Bradley, Konate, Gomez (C), Tsimikas (Robertson 66), Oxlade-Chamberlain, Jones (Henderson 87), Keita (Morton 46), Gordon, Origi, Minamino.
Subs not used: Adrian, Jota, Phillips, Balagizi.

PRESS BOX: NEIL JONES, GOAL.COM
"Playing on the right of Liverpool's attack – the space usually reserved for Mo Salah – Kaide Gordon's quality was apparent from the word go. His touch is immaculate, his balance too, and for one so young there is a pleasing appetite for the dirty side of the game too."

PUNDIT: GRANT HOLT, SKY SPORTS
"Kaide Gordon's movements, the way he moves, he's a bit like Mo Salah the way he goes down the line, he can take you inside, he can take you outside. He's got that movement about him. If you're in a football club like Liverpool and you've got Salah and Mane in those positions and you've someone like him looking at them, watching them, training round them, his pathway is going to be great."

REPORT:

The Reds opened their 2021/22 Premier League campaign with a 3-0 victory at Norwich City on the opening weekend of the season and enjoyed it so much that they went back to Carrow Road to do it all over again, this time in the Carabao Cup third round.

Of course, the team that Jürgen Klopp fielded was different to the starting XI that had played in the top-flight encounter, but the end-result was still the same.

Three teenagers made their debuts – right-back Conor Bradley and forward Kaide Gordon from the start, midfielder Tyler Morton from the bench – with Ibrahima Konate making his first appearance in an away match for the Reds while Joe Gomez captained Liverpool for the first time.

"It was a massive honour," Gomez told liverpoolfc.com afterwards. "Obviously after the period I've had, the different injuries and coming back, I'm relishing every minute and on top of that, to be able to captain the side was unbelievable. I really enjoyed it."

Much of the focus was on 16-year-old Gordon, who became Liverpool's fifth youngest-ever player on the night. But it was the other two members of the front-three, Divock Origi and Takumi Minamino, who combined to put Klopp's men ahead in the fourth minute.

Origi forced a corner and from a Kostas Tsimikas outswinger, he climbed above Canaries skipper Grant Hanley to knock the ball down to Minamino, who swivelled in the six-yard box and fired a low shot between the legs of Angus Gunn.

It was Minamino's fifth goal for Liverpool and his fifth away from home, setting a rather random club record of the most goals scored by a player who has never netted at Anfield. The previous joint-

→

18
44
LOTUS

44

17
standard chartered
LOTUS
sky sports

record holders, with four away goals apiece, were Fabio Aurelio and Jordon Ibe.

Less than 10 minutes later another Tsimikas corner found the head of League Cup debutant Konate, but the big French defender headed narrowly over. Then the travelling Kop got their first glimpse of what Gordon is all about.

After combining well with Bradley down the right he cut inside, shrugged off the attentions of Billy Gilmour and struck a left-footed shot that flashed past the diving Gunn at his near post.

As the half wore on the Reds lack of a natural defensive midfielder – Curtis Jones played in the role for the first time on his 50th Liverpool appearance – began to show and Norwich created chances.

Christos Tzolis headed over and Adam Idah had a shot saved by Caoimhin Kelleher, but when the Reds keeper could only parry another Tzolis effort in the 42nd minute, Bradley fouled Dimitris Giannoulis as the pair challenged for the rebound and referee Darren England pointed to the spot.

Designated penalty-taker Idah grabbed the ball, but 19-year-old Greek striker Tzolis wrestled it off him and stepped up to the spot instead, infuriating his manager Daniel Farke.

He struck it down the middle but Kelleher, who had dived to his right, produced a remarkable 'rabona' penalty save with the leg he had pushed off from. Gomez scrambled to block two shots from the rebound before Liverpool counter-attacked and almost made it 2-0 only for Jones' deflected shot to graze the roof of the net.

It was a game-changing intervention from Kelleher and at half-time Klopp took the opportunity to bring Morton on for the injured Naby Keita. The kid from the Wirral may have been a debutant, but he gave the midfield more balance and five minutes into the second stanza it was 2-0.

Jones worked the ball to the overlapping Tsimikas on the left and from his cross a completely unmarked Origi headed the ball past Gunn.

It was the Belgian's tenth League Cup goal, making him the ninth Liverpool player to reach double-figures in the competition, and he almost got his 11th when Gordon played him in behind the Canaries' defence only to curl a low shot wide of the far-post.

A third goal finally arrived in the 80th minute. Bradley, the first Northern Irish player to appear from Liverpool since 1954, won a tackle, Alex Oxlade-Chamberlain nudged the ball into Minamino's path and after delaying his shot to evade Andrew Omobamidele as he committed himself to a challenge, the Japanese international again beat Gunn with a low shot from close-range.

The Reds were on the road to Wembley and the next stop was much closer to home.

NORWICH	STATS	LIVERPOOL
47	POSSESSION (%)	53
12	SHOTS	17
5	SHOTS ON TARGET	3
1	CORNERS	8
3	OFFSIDES	2
18	CLEARANCES	5

MANAGER: JÜRGEN KLOPP
"Taki is in a good moment, trained really well and deserved these two goals. The first one, really good awareness, quick in mind, finished the situation off. The second one, the acceleration in the box in the short, small space was really good. The kids did exceptionally well too, I have to say. All three, physically really strong and that's maybe the biggest surprise, that they could go 92 minutes. I am really happy for them, it was a big moment for the boys."

FOR THE RECORD:
Norwich City goalkeeper Angus Gunn's father Bryan was in goal the last time the two clubs met in a cup tie: an FA Cup fourth-round replay at Anfield in 1990. Liverpool won 3-1.

ALSO THIS ROUND:
Manchester City 6 Wycombe Wanderers 1
QPR 2 Everton 2 (QPR win 8-7 on pens)
Manchester United 0 West Ham United 1
Chelsea 1 Aston Villa 1 (Chelsea win 4-3 on pens)

PRESTON NORTH END 0
LIVERPOOL 2

Goals: Minamino (62), Origi (84)

27.10.21 • Deepdale • Attendance: 22,131

Referee: David Coote

PRESTON (3-4-1-2): Rudd, van den Berg, Lindsay, A Hughes, Rafferty, McCann (Johnson 78), Ledson (Whiteman 79), Cunningham (C) (Earl 69), Potts, Barkhuizen (Riis 63), Maguire (Sinclair 79).
Subs not used: Iversen, Bauer, Storey, Huntington.

LIVERPOOL (4-3-3): Adrian, N Williams, Matip (Phillips 46), Gomez (C), Tsimikas, Oxlade-Chamberlain (Dixon-Bonner 90), Morton, Jones (Beck 90), Blair (Bradley 55), Origi, Minamino.
Subs not used: L Hughes, Pitaluga, Konate, Firmino, Jota.

PRESS BOX: IAN DOYLE, LIVERPOOL ECHO
"After the feast in recent weeks, the law of averages suggested a forgettable encounter was due, Liverpool's run of scoring at least three times in successive away games coming to an end at nine. No matter. With Man City dumped out at West Ham, the Carabao Cup has become an increasingly possible route to silverware for Klopp's side."

PUNDIT: ANDY HINCHCLIFFE, SKY SPORTS
"It's not been a great team performance by Liverpool but Neco Williams has played in two positions tonight and played well. Individually he's done so well. He's been involved in both goals, and he had the goal-line clearance in the first half to keep Liverpool afloat. He's had a very good night having come back from injury."

RED OCTOBER

MANAGER: JÜRGEN KLOPP

"We didn't play particularly well to be 100 per cent honest and Preston played long balls. They were tricky to defend and they had their moments. The game was open and we lost our structure in the first half which never helps in football. Divock showed his skills for the second but Preston played a really inspired game and the atmosphere was nice. No one got injured so it's a perfect night."

FOR THE RECORD:

Preston North End became the 70th different club that Liverpool have faced in the League Cup and this was also the 70th meeting between the two clubs in all competitions.

ALSO THIS ROUND:

West Ham 0 Manchester City 0 (West Ham win 5-4 on pens)
Arsenal 2 Leeds United 0
Burnley 0 Tottenham Hotspur 1
Chelsea 1 Southampton 1 (Chelsea win 4-3 on pens)

REPORT:

If there is one set of away supporters who feel at home on Deepdale's Bill Shankly Kop it is Liverpool's and just over 5,000 Reds were in Preston to see Takumi Minamino and Divock Origi see off the Championship challengers.

Make no mistake about it, though, this fourth-round tie was no walk in the park.

Liverpool had beaten Manchester United 5-0 at Old Trafford in the Premier League four days prior, but Jürgen Klopp made eleven changes and his side struggled for rhythm despite dominating possession.

An injury to Kaide Gordon opened the door for 18-year-old forward Harvey Blair to make his debut, becoming the 74th different player Klopp has selected in his 20th League Cup game as manager. Nat Phillips would make it 75, Elijah Dixon-Bonner 76 and debutant

PHILLIPS
17
Expedia
TSIMIKAS
21
ADRIAN

PRESTON NE	STATS	LIVERPOOL
27	POSSESSION (%)	73
9	SHOTS	9
4	SHOTS ON TARGET	4
4	CORNERS	1
2	OFFSIDES	0
10	CLEARANCES	13

Owen Beck 77 before the night was over, but there was also the unusual situation of a Liverpool player on the opposite team.

Dutch defender Sepp van der Berg, on loan at Preston for the second time, was given permission to play for the Lillywhites. "Of course he should play," said assistant-manager Pep Lijnders. "If you want to be a chef, you need to spend a lot of time in the kitchen."

Joe Gomez skippered the Redmen again, Adrian made his first start of the season and after a dull opening 25 minutes it was the Liverpool keeper who made the first save of the game, pushing a Brad Potts shot over.

Quite how Frankie McAvoy's side didn't go ahead in the 28th minute he will never know. Gomez was robbed of possession and Alistair McCann centred for Sean Maguire, just seven yards out. Adrian produced a fine one-handed save to deny a certain goal before Neco Williams blocked Ryan Ledson's follow-up shot on the goal-line with his face and Potts blazed the rebound over.

It was a remarkable let off for Liverpool and the half ended with the Reds having created pretty much nothing bar a couple of blocked Alex Oxlade-Chamberlain efforts. Improvement was needed.

Joel Matip was replaced by Phillips at the interval and moments after Oxlade-Chamberlain flashed a 25-yard shot past the post, Klopp decided another change was needed. Blair came off, Conor Bradley came on at right-back and Williams was sent up to play as a right-sided forward.

The Liverpool manager's tactical change paid dividends as just seven minutes later it led to the deadlock being broken. Tyler Morton spread the ball wide with a lovely diagonal pass to Williams, who cut inside the penalty area and clipped a cross to the near-post where Minamino flicked the ball past Declan Rudd with his left shin.

It was an improvised finish by Minamino, but Origi took improvisation to a whole new level in the 84th minute.

Kostas Tsimikas bent a cross into the Preston box but slightly over hit it and the ball hit the crossbar. Williams reacted quickest to reach the rebound, but his shot was blocked and the ball deflected across goal, behind Origi.

Scoring looked impossible, but Divock seemingly doesn't know the meaning of the word and flicked out his right leg to produce an audacious back-heeled scorpion-kick that looped the ball over his own head and the despairing dive of Rudd. It was Origi at his outrageous yet instinctive best.

"That goal was unbelievable and that's just what Divock can do," reflected MOTM Williams. "For me, he is one of the best finishers in the club. When you're training and playing with him week-in, week-out, you see the quality he brings and the finishes he produces in training.

"That's just what Divock does."

PNE were done-for and as stoppage-time approached, Klopp took the opportunity to bring on midfielder Dixon-Bonner and give left-back Beck, a nephew of Ian Rush no less, his first-team debut.

That it was only Liverpool's tenth victory in 35 visits to Deepdale was a reminder of what a difficult venue this has historically been to win at for the Reds, but it was also a show of squad strength that Klopp's men were now through to the quarter-finals without Alisson, Trent Alexander-Arnold, Virgil van Dijk, Fabinho, James Milner, Thiago, Harvey Elliott, Roberto Firmino, Sadio Mane, Mo Salah or Diogo Jota having kicked a ball in the competition.

They hadn't played at Anfield either, but that was about to change.

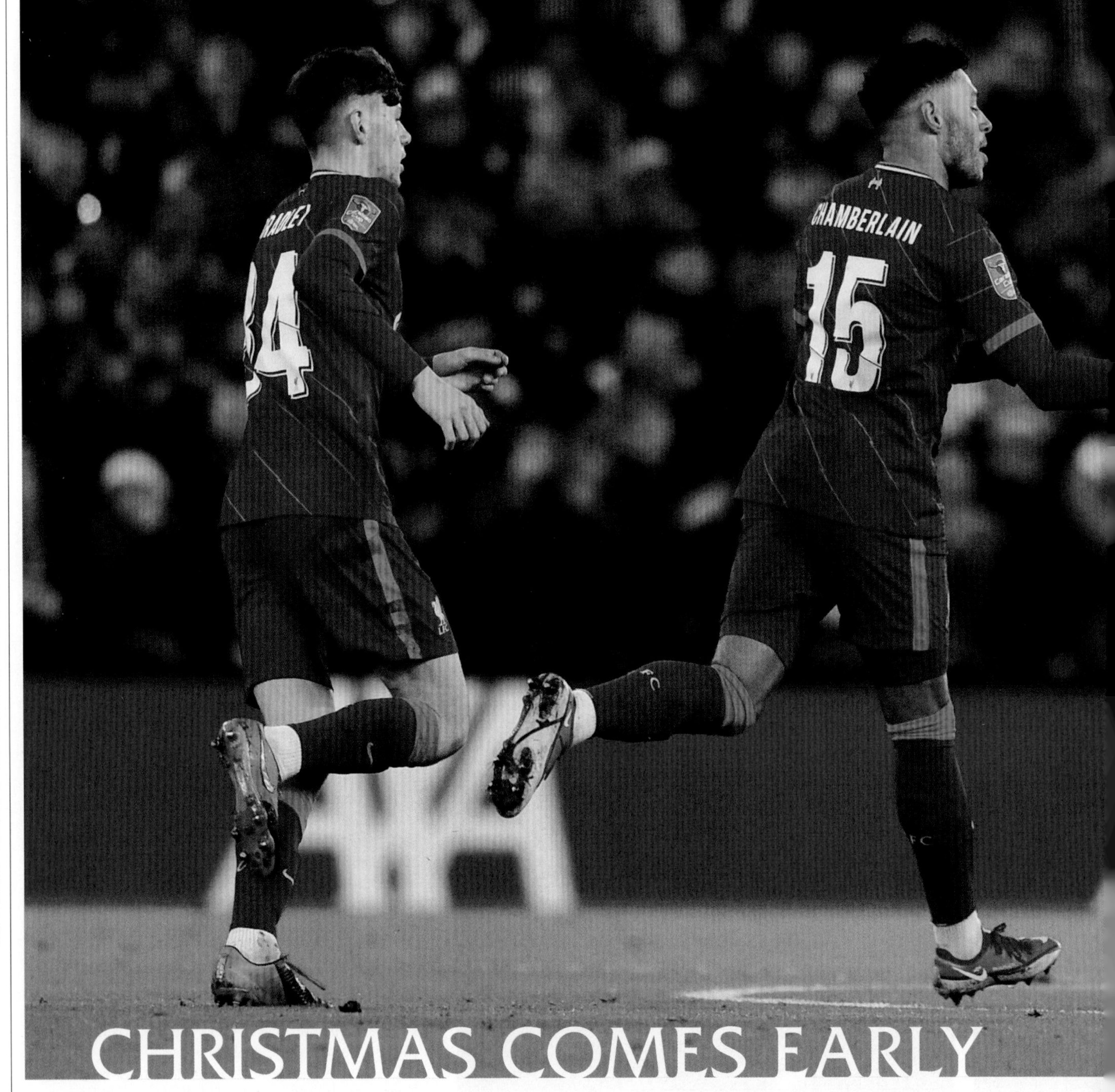

CHRISTMAS COMES EARLY

Liverpool win 5-4 on penalties

LIVERPOOL 3
LEICESTER CITY 3

Goals: Vardy (9, 13), Oxlade-Chamberlain (19), Maddison (33), Jota (68), Minamino (90)

22.12.21 • Anfield • Attendance: 52,020

Referee: Andy Madley

LIVERPOOL (4-3-3): Kelleher, Bradley (Jota 46), Gomez, Koumetio (Konate 46), Tsimikas (Beck 80), Henderson (C) (Keita 59), Morton (Milner 46), Oxlade-Chamberlain, N Williams, Firmino, Minamino. Subs not used: Pitaluga, Gordon, Quansah, Woltman. Booked: Morton.

LEICESTER CITY (4-3-1-2): Schmeichel (C), Pereira (Albrighton 42), Ndidi, Soyuncu (Vestergaard 60), Thomas, Tielemans, Soumare, Dewsbury-Hall (Bertrand 60), Maddison, Vardy, Daka (Iheanacho 56). Subs not used: Stolarczyk, Perez, Mendy, Lookman, Nelson. Booked: Maddison, Thomas.

PRESS BOX: IAN LADYMAN, DAILY MAIL

"As he watched his side reel in Leicester by sheer force of will in the second half before downing them in a penalty shoot-out, Klopp will have taken just as much satisfaction as he would from just about anything else this season. For this is the culture he has created. Do not lie down. Do not lose. This is a club with his name written right through it. This is Klopp's Liverpool."

PUNDIT: ROB GREEN, BBC 5 LIVE

"If the fans come away from that and say they are not entertained and it doesn't mean anything then I don't know what does. It was really entertaining football but it was a proper cup tie played in a proper way. Both teams were vulnerable, both teams went for it."

MANAGER: JÜRGEN KLOPP
"To Liverpool supporters I don't know exactly the percentage how much we mean in comparison to other things in their lives, but it is a big one. And yes we feel that responsibility, but we feel much more the push we get from that to be honest. This club is so special and everything that we do is important. I love it so much. Honestly, if I had known how good this club is and how much we mean to each other I'd have wanted to be here much earlier. It's absolutely outstanding."

FOR THE RECORD:
Caoimhin Kelleher became the fifth and youngest Liverpool goalkeeper to win two penalty shoot-outs following Bruce Grobbelaar, Jerzy Dudek, Pepe Reina and Simon Mignolet.

ALSO THIS ROUND:
Arsenal 5 Sunderland 1
Tottenham Hotspur 2 West Ham United 1
Brentford 0 Chelsea 2

REPORT:

You could hear sharp intakes of breath when the team-sheets for this Carabao Cup quarter-final were released.

In keeping with his philosophy to give young players opportunities in this competition, Klopp named Caoimhin Kelleher, Conor Bradley, Billy Koumetio and Tyler Morton in his starting XI while Neco Williams was asked to channel his inner Gareth Bale and play as a right-sided forward.

Brendan Rodgers, on the other hand, wheeled out the big guns. Kasper Schmeichel, Ricardo Pereira, Caglar Soyuncu, Wilfred Ndidi, Youri Tielemans, Kiernan Desbury-Hall, James Maddison, Patson Daka and Jamie Vardy all started.

The Foxes' previous two Premier League games had been postponed under COVID-19 protocols so it was tricky for Klopp and his analysts to preempt what kind of side Rodgers would field. On paper, Leicester looked stronger and the opening 45 minutes suggested that they were.

Maddison found space between the lines in the ninth minute and slid a pass for Vardy to run in behind Koumetio and fire across Kelleher to open the scoring.

Morton was booked for a shuddering challenge on Pereira and three minutes later it was 2-0 when Dewsbury-Hall sent Daka away down the left and he centred the ball for Vardy to side-foot home.

→

It was the Leicester striker's tenth goal against LFC, making him only the 27th player to reach double-goalscoring figures against the Reds with no currently active player having netted more.

The away fans were in full voice but repeatedly chanted one particular song that infuriated the Anfield crowd. Perhaps it transmitted to the players as in the 19th minute the Reds hit back.

Williams headed a Kostas Tsimikas cross down to Roberto Firmino and he laid the ball back for Alex Oxlade-Chamberlain to rifle home from the edge of the box.

Game on, but Liverpool were architects of their own downfall in the 33rd minute. Williams couldn't control Bradley's pass and when a favourable bounce off Oxlade-Chamberlain sat up for Maddison, he hit a dipping strike over Kelleher from 25 yards out.

Vardy then came incredibly close to completing his hat-trick when he seized on an error by Joe Gomez and ran clear but rattled the inside of the post with his shot.

It was the escape that Liverpool needed and at half-time Klopp made a triple substitution, introducing Ibrahima Konate, James Milner and Diogo Jota for Bradley, Koumetio and Morton.

Naby Keita followed 15 minutes later.

All of a sudden the tempo got quicker, Leicester's goalscoring opportunities dried up and the Reds created four or five half-chances, but it took until the 68th minute to get a goal back.

Firmino won possession on the edge of the Foxes box, Takumi Minamino played a cute pass around the corner and Jota took a touch before lashing a left-footed shot beyond Schmeichel. The rain began to pour and the Kop began to roar.

Tsimikas had three shots blocked as Leicester scrambled to clear a corner, Oxlade-Chamberlain fired over, Williams hit the side netting and Keita unleashed a piledriver that Jota deflected goalwards with his head only for Schmeichel to produce a brilliant save.

When Keita's shot was blocked in the fourth minute of stoppage-time and a penalty appeal for handball was correctly waved away by referee Andy Madley – as chants of Que Sera, Sera rang around the away end – it felt like Liverpool's Carabao Cup run was over. But these Reds never quit.

Williams won a throw-in and with Leicester preoccupied by a Gomez dummy-run, he threw it to Milner. The vice-skipper curled a cross to

LIVERPOOL	STATS	LEICESTER
66	POSSESSION (%)	34
22	SHOTS	8
6	SHOTS ON TARGET	7
15	CORNERS	2
2	OFFSIDES	2
7	CLEARANCES	37

the edge of the penalty area that was misjudged by Ndidi. Lurking behind him was Minamino and he chested the ball down before firing it past Schmeichel on the half-volley.

Several of the Leicester players collapsed to the turf in anguish and moments later, as Fields of Anfield Road rang out, the fill-time whistle went. Penalties.

Foxes skipper Schmeichel won both tosses and chose the Anfield Road end and for Leicester to take first.

Tielemans scored, Milner levelled. Maddison scored, Firmino levelled. Marc Albrighton scored, Oxlade-Chamberlain levelled. Then came the drama.

Kelleher dived to his left to deny Luke Thomas, Keita put Liverpool ahead. Kelechi Iheanacho levelled, Minamino had the chance to win it...but blazed over. Sudden death, but Kelleher was on it.

He dived to his left again to save from Ryan Bertand and then up stepped Jota...get in! Diogo celebrated wildly with an Anfield crowd that, like the team they support, never gave up.

Now bring on the Arsenal...

LIVERPOOL 0
ARSENAL 0

13.01.22 • Anfield • Attendance: 52,377
Referee: Michael Oliver

LIVERPOOL (4-3-3): Alisson, Alexander-Arnold (N Williams 76), Matip (Gomez 76), van Dijk, Robertson, Henderson (C), Fabinho (Oxlade-Chamberlain 75), Milner (Jones 71), Jota, Firmino, Minamino. Subs not used: Kelleher, Konate, Tsimikas, Gordon, Morton. Booked: Robertson.

ARSENAL (4-4-2): Ramsdale, Soares (Chambers 11), White, Gabriel, Tierney, Saka (Tavares 81), Lokonga, Xhaka, Martinelli, Lacazette (C), Nketiah (Holding 28). Subs not used: Leno, Mari, Biereth, Oulad M'Hand, Hutchinson, Patino. Booked: Gabriel. Sent off: Xhaka.

PRESS BOX: IAN KENNEDY, BBC RADIO MERSEYSIDE
"With almost 80 per cent possession, Liverpool could manage only one shot on target. They struggled to get anything going upfront, couldn't get in behind Arsenal's back-line often enough. Definitely an off-night, and the absences of Salah and Mane were only too apparent."

PUNDIT: PAUL MERSON, SKY SPORTS
"The biggest worry tonight if I were a Liverpool fan? Salah and Mane. If they play tonight, it's a different story. You can take two players out of Manchester City's team, doesn't really make a difference. Take two out of Chelsea, not really. Take two out of Liverpool, it's completely different."

NEW YEAR'S DISILLUSION

MANAGER: JÜRGEN KLOPP
"We would've preferred to have scored the goal instead of them getting a red card. From that moment it looks like we felt under pressure to score. We were not creative enough, definitely. We did a lot of things that were not good enough, but it's a two-legged game and it's half-time."

FOR THE RECORD:
Alisson made his League Cup debut to become the 79th different player used in this competition by Jürgen Klopp.

ALSO THIS ROUND:
Chelsea 2 Tottenham Hotspur 0 →

Emirates
AFC

sky

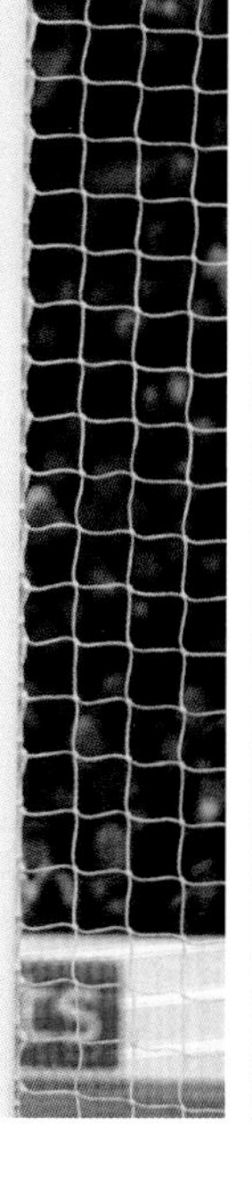

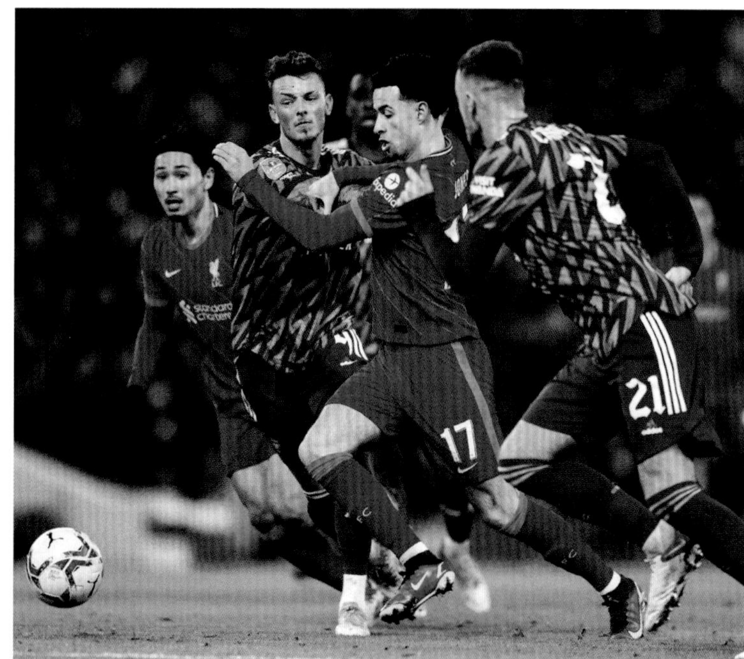

REPORT:

It wasn't so much Carabao Cup fever but COVID-19 that swept through the Liverpool camp before the first leg of the semi-final against Arsenal.

The Reds should have travelled to London a week earlier to face the Gunners, but with the highly infectious Omicron variant in circulation an outbreak among Jürgen Klopp's players and staff was so bad that the AXA Training Centre was closed – after consultation with the local public-health authority – and the club was forced to ask the EFL for a postponement.

It was frustrating, but as Arsenal fans discovered later in the month when their club asked for the North London derby at Tottenham to be postponed for similar reasons, sometimes circumstances are beyond your control.

So the most played League Cup fixture in history – this was the 13th meeting between these clubs and the third in consecutive seasons – finally got underway a week later than scheduled with the venues for each leg reversed after the postponement. Truth be told, it wasn't worth the wait.

Sometimes a 0-0 scoreline doesn't reflect a chance-filled game when both goalkeepers had worldies. Sometimes a 0-0 scoreline does what it says on the tin, so to speak. This was most definitely one of those latter occasions.

The only real opportunity of note during an opening 20 minutes in which Arsenal lost Cederic Soares through injury came when Ben White diverted Takumi Minamino's cross narrowly past his own post.

In the 24th minute Jordan Henderson got back to intercept a Bukayo Saka cross that Alexandre Lacazette was eyeing up and it led to the game-changing moment.

Alisson cleared, Roberto Firmino played the ball out wide to Andy Robertson and from his diagonal pass Diogo Jota had a clear run on

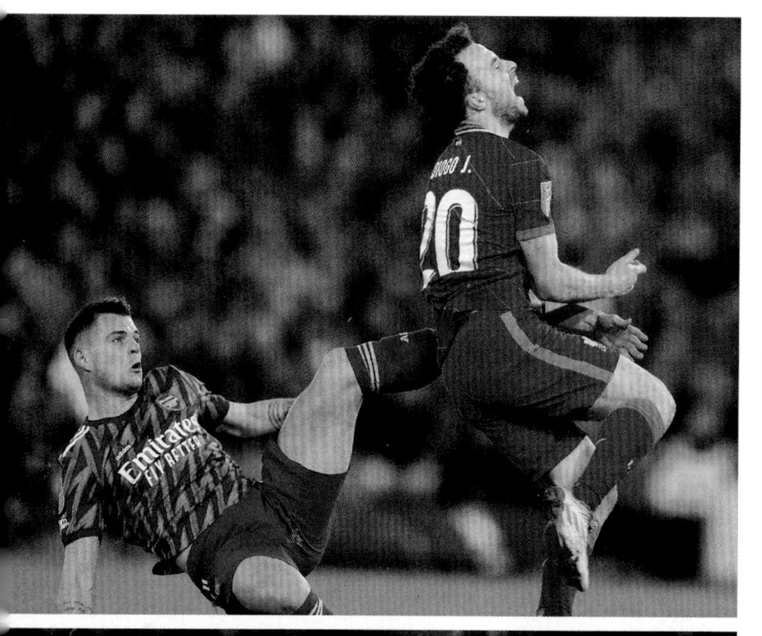

goal, but as he controlled the ball with his chest on the edge of the box he was booted in the midriff by Granit Xhaka.

Jota hit the deck and referee Michael Oliver immediately reached into his back pocket and produced a red card. Arsenal could have no complaints and manager Mikel Arteta reacted by substituting striker Eddie Nketiah, bringing on central defender Rob Holding and reverting to a 5-3-1 formation with Lacazette dropping in to make it a 5-4-0 when defending.

To have a man advantage for 66 minutes gave Liverpool an opportunity to put the Gunners under real pressure, but Xhaka's dismissal proved to be a false positive for the Reds. Like marmots in the winter months, Arsenal dug in and with each shot that Liverpool failed to get on target it increasingly felt like Groundhog Day.

Concerns about how the Reds would deal without Sadio Mane and Mo Salah while they were away at the Africa Cup of Nations grew, but not having Naby Keita or the injured Thiago to call upon in midfield didn't help either.

A slice of luck would have been useful and Minamino almost got one in the second half. He pounced on a loose ball and sprinted away from Calum Chambers down the left before trying to cross towards Firmino, only to slice the ball and send it looping over the despairing dive of Aaron Ramsdale – who was relieved to see it drop wide of his far-post.

Minamino flashed another shot across goal, from Robertson's pass, and substitute Curtis Jones had an on-target shot blocked, but then Alisson – making his League Cup debut as Jürgen Klopp felt he needed a game after recovering from COVID – did brilliantly to deny Saka with his knee as the ten men had a rare foray forward.

Joe Gomez, Alex Oxlade-Chamberlain and Neco Williams all came on and in the 90th minute the three combined to create the best chance of the whole game. Gomez played the ball wide to Williams, who found Oxlade-Chamberlain, and from his chipped cross Ramsdale clattered into his own man as he tried to punch the ball clear.

It fell to Minamino, 10 yards from goal, but he got underneath his attempted shot and skewed it high into the Kop, prompting frustrated groans as Gunners centre-back White celebrated on the goalline with two clenched fists.

White then had to block a low Williams drive after Ramsdale again made a mess of a punch when challenging Virgil van Dijk in the air from Jones' cross and moments later the final whistle blew.

Ten-man Arsenal had a 0-0 draw to take back to London and as their travelling fans sang about going to Wembley they must have felt like it was half the job done, but Liverpool had other ideas...

STATS

LIVERPOOL		ARSENAL
78	POSSESSION (%)	22
17	SHOTS	3
1	SHOTS ON TARGET	1
8	CORNERS	1
4	OFFSIDES	1
11	CLEARANCES	46

WEM-BER-LEE! WEM-BER-LEE!

ARSENAL 0
LIVERPOOL 2

Goals: Jota (19, 77)
20.01.22 • Emirates Stadium • Attendance: 59,360
Referee: Martin Atkinson

ARSENAL (4-1-4-1): Ramsdale, Tomiyasu, White, Gabriel, Tierney, Lokonga, Saka, Odegaard, Smith-Rowe (Partey 74), Martinelli, Lacazette (C) (Nketiah 74). Subs not used: Hein, Holding, Tavares, Alebiousu, Biereth, Oulad M'hand, Patino. Booked: Lacazette, Tomiyasu, Partey. Sent off: Partey.

LIVERPOOL (4-3-3): Kelleher, Alexander-Arnold, Matip (Konate 46), van Dijk, Robertson, Henderson (C) (Milner 75), Fabinho, Jones, Gordon (Minamino 63), Firmino (N Williams 84), Jota. Subs not used: Alisson, Adrian, Gomez, Tsimikas, Morton. Booked: Konate, Jones, Minamino.

PRESS BOX: PAUL GORST, LIVERPOOL ECHO
"No Mane, no Salah, no problem; Liverpool are heading to Wembley. And in some style, too. Arsenal fans left Anfield last week celebrating like their place in the Carabao Cup final was already safe after a dour goalless affair on Merseyside. 'We're going to Wembley!' they cooed as they started the journey back down south, clearly believing that this second leg was a foregone conclusion. Diogo Jota, though, had other ideas here at the Emirates."

PUNDIT: JAMIE REDKNAPP, SKY SPORTS
"Diogo Jota is such an intelligent footballer. I was so impressed with his game today. He looked like a man who thought: I'm going to show what I'm capable of. It was his time. He started the game well and it made the difference. Everything he did today was magnificent."

MANAGER: JÜRGEN KLOPP
"What the boys put out tonight was really special. I saw so many outstanding performances tonight in a very important game against a really strong Arsenal side. We really put a lot of effort in this competition and we really wanted to go through. So when you go through, when you're in the final, there's absolutely no reason to be part of a final if you don't want to win it. We want to win it but we know how difficult it will be."

FOR THE RECORD:
Kaide Gordon became the first 17-year-old, and youngest player, to appear in a semi-final for Liverpool during the club's history.

ALSO THIS ROUND:
Tottenham Hotspur 0 Chelsea 1

REPORT:

While it seemed like half the world was playing Wordle judging by the numbers sharing their scores on social media, the travelling Kop only had one five-letter word on their minds at The Emirates: DIOGO.

No Liverpool player had ever scored twice in a League Cup semi-final away from home before – Ronnie Whelan and Danny Murphy getting braces at Anfield in 1984 and 2001 respectively – so a small slice of history was created when a deadly Diogo double disarmed the Gunners and sent Jürgen Klopp's men to Wembley for a first cosmetic cup final since 2016.

With Sadio Mane, Mo Salah and Naby Keita still away at AFCON, an injury to the in-form Alex Oxlade-Chamberlain during the weekend Premier League win against Brentford was the last thing the Liverpool boss needed. But it opened the door for 17-year-old Kaide Gordon to start on the right.

Caoimhin Kelleher returned in goal and after the players emerged to flashing floodlights as Arsenal tried to whip up an atmosphere, it was the home side – with Takehiro Tomiyasu, Emile Smith-Rowe and Martin Odegaard all returning from injury – that had the early momentum.

A foul by Andy Robertson on Bukayo Saka on the edge of the box gave Alexandre Lacazette the chance to shoot, but Kelleher scampered across to his left to tip the ball onto the crossbar.

Liverpool, wearing their splendid all-yellow third strip to evoke memories of League Cup semi-finals at Burnley, Walsall and Southampton in the 1980s, began to grow into the game and had the ball in the net in the 13th minute.

Fabinho headed Robertson's corner back across goal and Joel Matip side-footed it in at the far-post, but the assistant referee's flag went up and the goal was chalked off. Six minutes later the Reds netted again and this time nobody was ruling it out.

Roberto Firmino's brilliant back-heel from Matip's pass found Trent Alexander-Arnold, who had moved inside into an advanced central midfield position. He slipped the ball to Jota on the left and the Portuguese international cut inside onto his right foot and hit a low, scuffed shot that went through Ben White's legs as he slid in, wrong-footing Aaron Ramsdale. Almost in slow motion, the ball rolled into the bottom corner.

The Reds were ahead and the 5,228 travelling Kopites behind the goal at the other end of The Emirates were soon in full voice as Creedence Clearwater Revival's Bad Moon Rising got a makeover.

'Oh he wears the number 20, he will take us to victory! And when he's running down the left wing, he'll cut inside and score for LFC! He's a lad from Portugal, better than Figo don't you know? Oh, his name is Diogo...'

Ibrahima Konate replaced Matip ahead of the second half, but rather than sit back and hold onto their 1-0 lead Liverpool went after more goals.

In the 51st minute Jota zipped past White down the left, cut into the box and pulled the ball back to Gordon. The teenager had intelligently run off the shoulder of Kieran Tierney to find space but blazed his shot into the travelling Kop.

Liverpool pressed on and when Ramsdale punched both the ball and, inadvertently, Tierney to concede a corner, Alexander-Arnold found Konate, but the big French centre-back's header thumped against the post.

Robertson flashed a 76th-minute shot wide, Arsenal brought on Thomas Partey – who had only returned from AFCON duty with Ghana that day – and with only one goal in it a nervous final 10 minutes appeared to be approaching until Alexander-Arnold and Jota combined again.

Liverpool's right-back played a glorious diagonal pass from the half-way line for Jota to chest down, shrug off White and dink the ball over Ramsdale as he dived at his feet.

Assistant referee Lee Betts' flag cut short the celebrations, but VAR had a look and spotted that Gabriel was playing him on so Martin Atkinson drew an imaginary rectangle and pointed to the halfway line. Arsenal 0 Liverpool 2 and Jota and his team-mates ran back down to the travelling Kop to celebrate.

Mikel Arteta's men looked beaten and when Partey, booked in the 87th minute for a foul on Neco Williams, hacked down Fabinho three minutes later he must have wished he hadn't got back from Cameroon so soon as he was heading to the dressing-room before his team-mates.

Liverpool, on the other hand, were heading to Wembley and as the travelling Kop headed out into the North London night they had a different five-letter word on their minds: FINAL.

STATS

ARSENAL		LIVERPOOL
46	POSSESSION (%)	54
7	SHOTS	11
2	SHOTS ON TARGET	3
5	CORNERS	2
4	OFFSIDES	3
16	CLEARANCES	17

THE FIRST EIGHT

Liverpool's previous League Cup triumphs have seen high drama, unlikely heroes, and plenty of memorable goals

THE FIRST TIME

1981 Liverpool 1 West Ham United 1 (aet); Liverpool 2 West Ham United 1

Four decades ago the Reds were favourites to beat West Ham, but the Londoners were ten points clear at the top of the Second Division and a tough afternoon for Bob Paisley's side could not be ruled out.

That proved to be the case with two hours of football at Wembley unable to separate the sides. With just three minutes of extra-time left, Alan Kennedy appeared to have won it. But Terry McDermott's habit of making headlines at Wembley continued as he handled a header from West Ham's Liverpool-born centre-back Alvin Martin on the line. In the battle of the Rays, right-back Stewart sent keeper Clemence the wrong way from the penalty-spot to send the tie to a Villa Park replay...

A fortnight later, goals from Kenny Dalglish and Alan Hansen secured Liverpool's first League Cup triumph. "On our way back from Villa Park, the cup was being handed around the coach and all talk was about where we would celebrate," captain Phil Thompson recalled. Suffice to say a good night was had by all.

"The next morning I received a call from Peter Robinson, our chief-executive, who asked where the trophy was. I told him it was on the bus. 'Yes I know', he replied. 'I've just had a call from the depot in St Helens — the driver found it on the back seat when he was cleaning up. Don't let the next one out of your sight!'"

EARNING OUR SPURS

1982 Liverpool 3 Tottenham Hotspur 1 (aet)

More late drama ensued in another tense final. Spurs, the FA Cup holders, led through a Steve Archibald goal after eleven minutes, and only a goal-line clearance by Graeme Souness prevented Archibald doubling the advantage.

That intervention proved crucial when Ronnie Whelan equalised three minutes from the end. Before extra-time began Bob Paisley urged his men to stand up to show Tottenham that they weren't tired.

Whether that tactic had any effect will remain unknown, but what is certain is that Liverpool were the better side in the additional period. Whelan again and an Ian Rush effort ensured the cup was retained.

"WHELAN'S CURLED IT"

1983 Liverpool 2 Manchester United 1 (aet)

Once again Liverpool did it the hard way, falling behind to a Norman Whiteside goal in the first half. Alan Kennedy's effort eluded goalkeeper Gary Bailey for the equaliser and the left-back later revealed how some of his team-mates were laughing when he scored because they thought the shot was so badly-struck.

The by-now familiar period of extra-time eventually led to Liverpool wearing down an injury-hit United. Whelan curled in a beautiful winner and Bob Paisley was memorably ushered up the famous steps by his players to collect the cup in his final final at the helm.

DERBY DELIGHT

1984 Liverpool 0 Everton 0 (aet); Liverpool 1 Everton 0

By the mid-Eighties Liverpool's players must have thought the League Cup final was a mandatory game of 120 minutes.

Everton probably edged proceedings in the first all-Merseyside Wembley final, with Alan Hansen's handling of Adrian Heath's shot on the line after just seven minutes going unpunished.

Not even Liverpool's usual Wembley goalscorers of the previous years, Rush and Kennedy, could influence the outcome: the former missed the target from almost under the crossbar and the latter had a goal disallowed.

Three days later Graeme Souness was captain and match-winner in the Maine Road replay. "It was a great occasion for the city of Liverpool to have two teams in the final," he remembered. "It meant a lot to people.

"We were very lucky to come away from the first game with a draw – there were some harsh words exchanged at half-time.

"The replay was dour but memorable for me as I scored. I miscontrolled it and had my back to goal but flashed a leg at it and it just dipped in front of Everton keeper Neville Southall before going in.

"It was a bit ad-hoc when we were presented with the trophy. A fan got in the way between me and Bruce Grobbelaar as I passed it down the line, but it was all good fun."

THE McMANAMAN FINAL
1995 Liverpool 2 Bolton Wanderers 1

Steve McManaman bewitched Bolton with a couple of stunning solo goals as the Reds claimed a record fifth League Cup triumph.

His first arrived eight minutes before the break when he ran on to a John Barnes pass, drifted outside Alan Stubbs and inside Scott Green before side-footing past goalkeeper Keith Branagan.

Midway through the second half another successful slalom saw him ghost past Green, Jason McAteer and Mark Seagraves before curling a low right-footed shot beyond Branagan.

Alan Thompson hooked in a reply for the Football League side but it was Liverpool captain Ian Rush who lifted the trophy.

WORTHY WINNERS

2001 Liverpool 1 Birmingham City 1
(aet; 5-4 pens)

A tense occasion saw the Reds win the first of an eventual cup treble in Cardiff. Defender Darren Purse equalised for Birmingham after Robbie Fowler's spectacular early opener. Andy Johnson later missed the decisive penalty. Jamie Carragher had scored his spot-kick moments before.

"It was sudden death but I didn't have any nerves," Carra said. "I knew where I wanted to put it and thankfully it went in. My dad missed the moment, though – he left his seat because he couldn't watch.

"It had been a difficult game but we battled through and deserved it. It was my first trophy with the senior Liverpool team and it was the catalyst for us to go on and win the cup treble.

"Gerard Houllier told us to remember how winning felt and urged us to use it as an inspiration. It was and we did."

JERZY'S BOYS

2003 Liverpool 2 Manchester United 0

Liverpool clinched their seventh League Cup final win at the Millennium Stadium in Cardiff thanks to goals from Steven Gerrard and Michael Owen.

Goalkeeper Jerzy Dudek, who made some costly errors against United in a league game at Anfield a couple of months earlier, was nominated man of the match.

"I told Jerzy three days ago, 'I can feel you will be the hero'," boss Gerard Houllier said afterwards. "Today he was man-of-the-match but football can be like that. Sometimes you can be at the bottom and then be a hero again.

"I just had a feeling. I'm a great believer that when you have the right attitude everything else follows. He had a good run after the World Cup but then he made some mistakes and we had to support him."

CARLING THE SHOTS

2012 Liverpool 2 Cardiff City 2 (aet; 3-2 pens)

Kenny Dalglish guided the Reds to their eighth League Cup triumph in a final that saw Championship side Cardiff push Liverpool all the way.

Joe Mason's first-half opener gave the Welsh side a half-time advantage which was cancelled out by Martin Skrtel on the hour-mark. With no further scoring the game went into extra-time and Dirk Kuyt's goal seemed to have secured the silverware for the Reds. But with two minutes of over-time remaining, centre-back Ben Turner pulled the Bluebirds level and took the game to a shoot-out.

Steven Gerrard, Kenny Miller and Charlie Adam missed the first three kicks and when Don Cowie slotted home, things appeared to be going Cardiff's way. But Kuyt converted his pen and Rudy Gestede struck a post – leaving things level after three efforts each.

Stewart Downing and Peter Whittingham netted and Glen Johnson then stroked home the Reds' fifth. Anthony Gerrard, cousin of Steven, had to score to send it to sudden death but fired wide leaving Dalglish and the Reds to celebrate another piece of silverware.

JUST BOSS

Jürgen Klopp has become the sixth manager to lead Liverpool to League Cup glory, joining a handful of illustrious names from the club's silver-lined history

BOB PAISLEY 1981, 1982, 1983

Bob led Liverpool to their first League Cup triumphs in the early 1980s as the Reds finally claimed the distinctive three-handled trophy.

He took charge in 53 League Cup ties, winning 32, drawing 13 and losing eight. Under his stewardship Liverpool scored 98 times in League Cup clashes, conceding 31.

In four finals under his watch they won three times, against West Ham, Tottenham and Manchester United, for the latter in March 1983 climbing Wembley's famous steps to collect the trophy in what was his last major final in charge.

His three League Cup triumphs were among 20 trophies he won in nine seasons – not bad for a man who was initially loath to make the step into football management.

A humble son of the North East, he was always more at ease in the wings rather than centre-stage. But when it came to knowledge of the game and the ability to spot a player, his record spoke volumes.

Kenny Dalglish, Alan Hansen, Graeme Souness, Alan Kennedy, Ronnie Whelan, Ian Rush and Mark Lawrenson were just some of the players brought to Anfield during his time in charge and each went on to cement themselves as a club legend.

In the process, three European Cups, six league titles and one UEFA Cup – as well as those three League Cups – were added to the Anfield honours board.

His achievements in such a short period in charge cannot be overstated and he is quite rightly recognised as one of the greatest football managers of all time.

JOE FAGAN 1984

'Smokin' Joe led the Reds to a fourth successive League Cup triumph when they saw off Everton after a replay at Maine Road following the clubs' first all-Merseyside Wembley final in 1984.

A quiet and effective worker behind the scenes, Joe's succession to the Anfield throne was the logical step after he had risen through the ranks under Bob Paisley following Bill Shankly's resignation in 1974.

Happily for Liverpool, he proved more than capable in the task, and in his debut season in charge that League Cup was the first part of an unprecedented treble which also included the league title and the European Cup.

The affable Scouser's second and final campaign at the helm concluded in tragic fashion at Heysel, as 39 supporters needlessly lost their lives. But that sad end did not harm the legacy of an important figure in LFC history.

Reds defender Mark Lawrenson said of him: "The biggest tribute I could pay to him would be when he got the job, every single man in the first-team squad were desperate for him to be successful.

"He was following a formidable act in Bob, and I think one or two different people outside of Liverpool thought maybe it was going to be too difficult an act to follow. But he was brilliant and we all really, really wanted him to be successful. That was obviously reflected in his first season."

Liverpool's League Cup triumph in the mid-1990s would prove to be the only trophy of Roy's reign as manager despite the team playing an attractive brand of attacking football.

A former England schoolboy international, he first moved to Anfield as an apprentice in 1965, progressing through the playing ranks before making the first of eleven senior appearances in 1970.

A much brighter future beckoned on the backroom staff, with Evans becoming the youngest coach to work in the Football League aged just 25 when he hung up his boots and accepted the position of reserve-team manager.

It was a role in which he shone, leading the second string to seven Central League titles in just nine years before stepping up to work with the first team.

During Roy's own eventual spell as manager, Liverpool lifted that League Cup and consistently finished in the top four of the Premier League.

On being made manager in 1994, he said: "I've been on this planet for 45 years and have supported Liverpool for 42 of them. The pride I feel is almost indescribable. I'm a Liverpool lad. I stood on the Kop as a youngster and understand the football expectations of all our supporters.

"It was almost 30 years ago when I was presented to manager Bill Shankly as a 15-year-old prospect and the respect I had for that man was ultimate. 'You are joining the greatest club in the world', he told me in his office. I believed him then, and I believe it now."

Between 1999 and 2004, 'Le Boss' managed the Reds in 18 League Cup ties, winning 13 and losing five. In winning the trophy on two occasions, his Liverpool side scored 50 goals and conceded 24.

The Frenchman was in charge of the Reds for six seasons, leading his team to an historic treble of League Cup, FA Cup and UEFA Cup in 2000/01 and returning the club to the Champions League.

Gerard recovered from life-saving heart surgery during the 2001/02 campaign to return to the dugout, and he later guided Liverpool to a second League Cup triumph in 2003. He departed the following year having overseen 307 matches and successfully re-establishing the club as a modern force.

Asked about his role as Reds manager, he said: "One, you run the team and the staff, you have responsibility for improving results and winning trophies. Two, you have an impact on the running of the club, helping build up the facilities. And three, you leave a legacy, to make sure the club will achieve in the future, whether it is with me or somebody else.

"Paisley had a better record than Shankly, but he completed what Shankly had built up.

"I don't believe in being 'Mr Motivator', more in creating the best environment for the players to fulfil their potential. Then it is up to their professionalism and desire to be winners."

SIR KENNY DALGLISH 2012

'The King' has the best statistical record of any Liverpool manager in terms of victories and goals scored in the League Cup.

Dalglish won a League Cup winner's medal as boss with the victory over Cardiff City a decade ago, having previously lost one final to Arsenal in 1987 – en route to which the Reds beat Fulham 10-0 in a second round first leg.

The legendary Scot managed Liverpool in 38 League Cup games, winning 24, drawing eight and losing six. During that time his sides scored 86 goals, conceding 36.

Considered by many as Liverpool's greatest player, his impact on the playing field had been nothing short of sensational. In the aftermath of the Heysel tragedy, the club hoped he could reproduce his genius in the dugout. It was a big ask for someone who was just 34 years old, but then Dalglish was not your average man.

His first season in charge as player-manager saw Liverpool win the League and FA Cup double for the only time in the club's history. He built on that success by assembling one of the most entertaining teams ever to grace Anfield, with two further league titles and another FA Cup subsequently added to his honours list before he stepped down in 1991.

A second spell between 2011 and 2012 brought that League Cup winner's medal that had previously eluded him as a manager.

LFC LEAGUE CUP MANAGERS RECORD

MANAGER	P	W	D	L	F	A	TROPHIES	FINALS LOST
BILL SHANKLY	30	13	9	8	51	35	0	0
BOB PAISLEY	53	32	13	8	98	31	3	1
JOE FAGAN	16	8	7	1	27	9	1	0
GRAEME SOUNESS	16	7	6	3	38	22	0	0
ROY EVANS	21	17	1	3	42	14	1	0
EVANS/HOULLIER	2	1	0	1	4	4	0	0
GERARD HOULLIER	18	13	0	5	50	24	2	0
RAFAEL BENITEZ	17	11	0	6	31	27	0	1
ROY HODGSON	1	0	0	1	2	2	0	0
KENNY DALGLISH	38	24	8	6	86	36	1	1
BRENDAN RODGERS	10	4	3	3	16	14	0	0
JÜRGEN KLOPP	24	13	5	6	46	25	1	1

LFC LEAGUE CUP APPEARANCES

Ian Rush	78
Bruce Grobbelaar	70
Alan Hansen	68
Phil Neal	66
Kenny Dalglish	59
Ray Clemence	55
Mark Lawrenson	50
Ronnie Whelan	50
Emlyn Hughes	46
Alan Kennedy	45
Graeme Souness	45
Phil Thompson	43
Ian Callaghan	42
Steve Nicol	42
Sammy Lee	39
Steve Heighway	38
Terry McDermott	36
Robbie Fowler	35
Craig Johnston	35
Ray Kennedy	35

LFC LEAGUE CUP GOALSCORERS

Ian Rush	48
Robbie Fowler	29
Kenny Dalglish	27
Ronnie Whelan	14
Steve McMahon	13
Danny Murphy	11
Divock Origi	11
David Fairclough	10
Steve McManaman	10
Steven Gerrard	9
David Johnson	9
Jan Molby	9
Michael Owen	9
Graeme Souness	9

KENNY DALGLISH 1981
It may have been before the 'official' man-of-the-match was awarded but Kenny got the nod from the press for his part in the replay victory against West Ham at Villa Park which saw the Reds win the trophy for the first time. His brilliant volley-on-the-turn opened the scoring.

LEAGUE CUP LEGENDS

From 1981 to 2012, the men in each winning LFC final who made a standout contribution to success